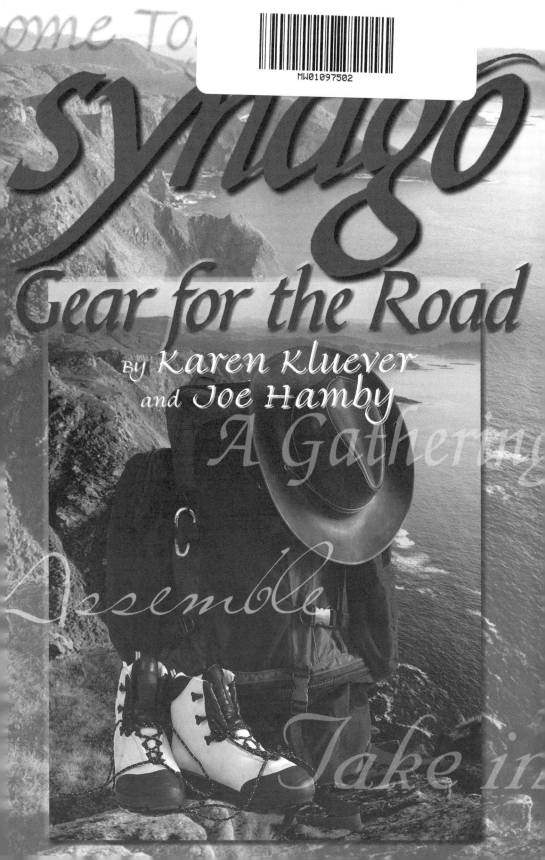

ome To

synago8

Gear for the Road

By Karen Kluever
and Joe Hamby

A Gathering

Assemble

Take in

Synago
Gear for the Road

© 2003 by Abingdon Press
All rights reserved.

Cover Design: Keely Moore

Scripture Credits

Contemporary English Version (CEV)
Scripture quotations marked (CEV) are from the Contemporary English Version copyright © 1991, 1992, 1995 by American Bible Society. Used by permission.

The Message (Message)
Scripture taken from THE MESSAGE. Copyright © Eugene H. Peterson, 1993, 1994, 1995. Used by permission of NavPress Publishing Group.

New Century Version (NCV)
Scriptures quoted from The Holy Bible, New Century Version, copyright © 1987, 1988, 1991 by Word Publishing, Nashville, Tennessee 37214. Used by permission.

New International Version (NIV)
Scripture quotations marked (NIV) are taken from the HOLY BIBLE, NEW INTERNATIONAL VERSION® NIV®. Copyright © 1973, 1978, 1984 by International Bible Society. Used by permission of Zondervan Publishing House. All rights reserved.

New Revised Standard Version (NRSV)
New Revised Standard Version of the Bible, copyright 1989, Divisions of Christian Education of the National Council of Churches of Christ in the United States of America. Used by permission. All rights reserved.

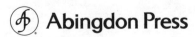

Abingdon Press

03 04 05 06 07 08 09 10 11 12—10 9 8 7 6 5 4 3 2 1

Contents

Sessions

Coming . . .

Benefits for You

BE-COMING A SMALL GROUP MEMBER

As a member of a small group, you can

- be with your friends and make new ones
- be yourself
- be encouraged
- be an explorer—of the Christian faith and the Bible
- be listened to
- be able to share thoughts, opinions, and feelings with peers
- be safe—everything's confidential!
- be introduced to a caring, Christian adult who's also a group member
- be challenged to live out new insights as part of a faith community
- be responsible—for caring for others, being open-minded, keeping confidences, and inviting friends
- be valued as a child of God!

And Growing

Multiplying the Benefits

GOING AND GROWING

A small group isn't a clique. It is open, inviting, and welcoming.

A small group grows as its members invite their friends. (Why would you keep such a great experience all to yourself? You've got to share it with others!)

When your small group gets to ten regular members, you'll want to "multiply" into two smaller groups. Think about it. If a small group grows and gets bigger and bigger, it's no longer a small, intimate group.

Although going, or "growing," from one group to two can be hard (people you've become close to may be in a different group), there are major benefits to multiplying:

- There's more time for everyone to participate in smaller groups; it's easier to start and end on time.

- Shy students are more likely to open up in a group of five than in a group of twelve.

- You can invite more friends, because you have room to grow.

- There's an opportunity for two more students to become group leaders; as groups multiply, new leaders are needed.

As a small group member, you should want your group to grow. Being in a small group is a great experience and one you'll want to share with friends and other students who need a place to feel accepted and loved.

When your group is ready to multiply, plan a "birth day" celebration. Keep the small-group experience growing and going.

Purpose Statement for Student-Led Small Groups

The purposes of our small group are to

- grow closer in our relationships with God and Jesus Christ;

- grow closer in our relationships with one another;

- learn more about the Christian faith and God's Word;

- encourage honesty and sharing in an atmosphere of trust, confidentiality, and open-mindedness;

- support one another and care for one another in Christian love;

- grow in number by inviting others;

- "multiply" into two groups when we reach 10 regular members to encourage intimacy and continued growth.

Confidentiality

Ground Rules

What's said in the group, stays in the group.

Confidentiality is critical to the small group experience.

For you and other group members to grow closer to one another and develop the special, intimate bonds of Christian friendship, you must be able to trust one another with personal information that is discussed in the group. This kind of trust is risky; but without it, no one will tell his or her true thoughts and feelings, and the group will not grow closer to one another.

Being honest requires being vulnerable, opening yourself up and exposing the real you. But you won't do this if you can't trust other group members not to spread around something you've told them. Likewise, you must keep to yourself anything of a personal nature that's shared by others in your small group. If you gossip or tell it to someone else outside the group, you break confidence, hurt someone in your group, and make your group an "unsafe" environment for others. Breaking confidentiality can be a deadly blow to a small group.

This is why confidentiality is included in the purpose statement for student-led small groups. This statement, read at the beginning of each small group session, reminds each person present to "encourage honesty and sharing in an atmosphere of trust, confidentiality, and open-mindedness."

- -

Colossians 3:1-17 (NIV)

(The Apostle Paul probably wrote this letter to the young church in Colossae while he was imprisoned in Rome. Paul wrote to the Colossian church to address false teachings, or heresy, in the church, such as angel worship; strict ritualistic rules; and a greater emphasis on human wisdom and tradition, rather than on Christ.)

Since, then, you have been raised with Christ, set your hearts on things above, where Christ is seated at the right hand of God. Set your minds on things above, not on earthly things. For you died, and your life is now hidden with Christ in God. When Christ, who is your life, appears, then you also will appear with him in glory.

Put to death, therefore, whatever belongs to your earthly nature: sexual immorality, impurity, lust, evil desires and greed, which is idolatry. Because of these, the wrath of God is coming. You used to walk in these ways, in the life you once lived. But now you must rid yourselves of all such things as these: anger, rage, malice, slander, and filthy language from your lips. Do not lie to each other, since you have taken off your old self with its practices and have put on the new self, which is being renewed in knowledge in the image of its Creator. Here there is no Greek or Jew, circumcised or uncircumcised, barbarian, Scythian, slave or free, but Christ is all, and is in all.

Therefore, as God's chosen people, holy and dearly loved, clothe yourselves with compassion, kindness, humility, gentleness and patience. Bear with each other and forgive whatever grievances you may have against one another. Forgive as the Lord forgave you. And over all these virtues put on love, which binds them all together in perfect unity.

Let the peace of Christ rule in your hearts, since as members of one body you were called to peace. And be thankful. Let the word of Christ dwell in you richly as you teach and admonish one another with all wisdom, and as you sing psalms, hymns and spiritual songs, with gratitude in your hearts to God. And whatever you do, whether in word or deed, do it all in the name of the Lord Jesus, giving thanks to God the Father through him.

Barbarians were people who didn't speak Greek and were considered low class and uncivilized; Sythians, originally from present-day south Russia, were infamous for their cruelty.

The city of Colossae was in Asia Minor, today's Turkey. Once a leading city in the region, by Paul's time, Colossae had lost a great deal of its former power, influence, and status to nearby towns.

8 "God's chosen people," traditionally a reference to the Hebrews, is used by Paul to describe the Christian community; he wants them to understand that the way they live must reflect their new identity.

"At the right hand," or on the right side, refers to being in a position of honor and power.

Notes

"Psalms" could have meant those psalms in the Hebrew Scriptures (Old Testament) or newly-written songs for Christian worship; "hymns" were praise songs, typically sung in celebration; "spiritual songs" described and praised God for specific things God had done.

Pray For

Next Meeting at

_____

Date

_____

R & R
REFLECT AND RESPOND

Read Colossians 3:1-17. In the space provided, list the "earthly clothes" and "Christ clothes" given in the reading. Then, check the ones you wear the most.

Earthly Clothes	Christ Clothes

Reread and think about the Colossians text. Write down the "clothing" that's the hardest for you to remove. Pray for God's help. If you aren't a Christian, how would you describe the "clothing" worn by the Christians you know?

As a prayer of meditation, slowly repeat the phrase "Chosen, holy, and dearly loved" (from verse 12) for several minutes. Repeat it to yourself daily, throughout the week, as a silent prayer and meditation.

Clean out your closet and drawers of clothes. Take out clothes you don't wear or rarely wear *and* clothes that do not honor God. Donate them to Goodwill or another charitable organization.

"Hidden with Christ" may mean being with Christ in heaven.

On the Outside, Lookin' in ------------------------------------

The Book of Acts reports the beginnings and growth of the Christian church. It tells about the activities of the early church leaders, particularly Paul, a persecutor of Christians who became one of the church's greatest missionaries.

Acts 9:26-29a (NCV)

When Saul went to Jerusalem, he tried to join a group of followers, but they were all afraid of him. They did not believe he was really a follower. But Barnabas accepted Saul and took him to the apostles. Barnabas explained to them that Saul had seen the Lord on the road and the Lord had spoken to Saul. Then he told them how boldly Saul had preached in the name of Jesus in Damascus.

1 Corinthians 12:12-18, 24b-27 (The Message)

(Paul is writing to the church in Corinth, where certain spiritual gifts, such as speaking in tongues, were considered more important than others, causing some church members who didn't have them to feel inferior. Paul deals with that issue in this passage.)

Your body has many parts—limbs, organs, cells—but no matter how many parts you can name, you're still one body. It's exactly the same with Christ. By means of his one Spirit, we all said goodbye to our partial and piecemeal lives. We each used to independently call our own shots, but then we entered into a large and integrated life in which *he* has the final say in everything. (This is what we proclaimed in word and action when we were baptized.) Each of us is now a part of his resurrection body, refreshed and sustained at one fountain—his Spirit—where we all come to drink. The old labels we once used to identify ourselves—labels like Jew or Greek, slave or free—are no longer useful. We need something larger, more comprehensive.

I want you to think about how all this makes you more significant, not less. A body isn't just a single part blown up into something huge. It's all the different-but-similar parts arranged and functioning together. . . . If the body was all eye, how could it hear? If all ear, how could it smell? As it is, we see that God has carefully placed each part of the body right where he wanted it. . . .

The way God designed our bodies is a model for understanding our lives together as a church: every part dependent on every other part, the parts we mention and the parts we don't, the parts we see and the parts we don't. If one part hurts, every other part is involved in the hurt, and in the healing. If one part flourishes, every other part enters into the exuberance.

You are Christ's body—that's who you are! You must never forget this.

"Saul" was Paul's Jewish name. Beginning in Acts 13:9, he's called Paul, h Roman name, possibly because he has starting his missionary ministry to Gentiles, or non-Jews. Read more about Paul in Acts 8:1-3 and 9:1-25.

After his conversion, Paul had to go to Jerusalem to talk to the early Christian leaders; these were Jesus' original disciples (plus the one who replaced Judas) and Jesus' brother James.

"You are Christ's body!" Paul's point is that each local church is the body of Christ, just as the universal church (the Christian church in the world) is also the body of Christ.

Notes

Pray for

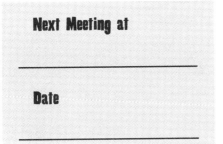

Next Meeting at

_____

Date

_____

Barnabas, whose name meant "Son of Encouragement," is first mentioned in Acts 4:36-37 for his generous giving to the newly-formed Christian community. He later became an important leader and teacher in the early church and companion to Paul in spreading the gospel to the Gentiles.

R & R
REFLECT AND RESPOND

Read Acts 9:26-29a. List the groups you belong to, including unofficial cliques or peer groups. In these groups, do you encourage an attitude of accepting others, a sense of belonging, and group unity? How? Or do you discourage those things? Why? Be honest. Ask God's help in accepting and caring for others.

Reread the passage from Acts. Who needs you to be his or her Barnabas?

Listen to this song about belonging:

"All I need is a place where I belong/A place where I can be the person God created me to be.

"All I need is a place to feel at home/Where I am loved and know that I belong."

—Karen Kluever

Is your small group a place where you belong? Where others belong? Pray for everyone in your group and for God's help to be a group where people feel accepted.

Pray for someone who needs a group like this. Invite him or her to yours.

In God We Trust?

Genesis 22:1-14 (CEV)

Some years later God decided to test Abraham, so he spoke to him.

Abraham answered, "Here I am, LORD."

The LORD said, "Go get Isaac, your only son, the one you dearly love! Take him to the land of Moriah, and I will show you a mountain where you must sacrifice him to me on the fires of an altar." So Abraham got up early the next morning and chopped wood for the fire. He put a saddle on his donkey and left with Isaac and two servants for the place where God had told him to go.

Three days later Abraham looked off in the distance and saw the place. He told his servants, "Stay here with the donkey, while my son and I go over there to worship. We will come back."

Abraham put the wood on Isaac's shoulder, but he carried the hot coals and the knife. As the two of them walked along, Isaac said, "Father, we have the coals and the wood, but where is the lamb for the sacrifice?"

"My son," Abraham answered, "God will provide the lamb.". . .

When they reached the place that God had told him about, Abraham built an altar and placed the wood on it. Next, he tied up his son and put him on the wood. He then took the knife and got ready to kill his son. But the LORD'S angel shouted from heaven, "Abraham! Abraham!"

"Here I am!" he answered.

"Don't hurt the boy or harm him in any way!" the angel said. "Now I know that you truly obey God, because you were willing to offer him your only son."

Abraham looked up and saw a ram caught by its horns in the bushes. So he took the ram and sacrificed it in place of his son.

Abraham named that place "The LORD Will Provide." And even now people say, "On the mountain of the Lord it will be provided."

The birth of Isaac to Abraham and his wife, Sarah, fulfilled a promise God had made to the couple. Even though the two were old and Sarah had not been able to have children, God had promised them a child. In the covenant, or agreement, God made with Abraham, he and his descendants were to be God's chosen people; in exchange for their faithfulness to God as the one and only God, God would give them the land of Canaan and would always be with them.

Although "boy" could refer to a male at any age from infancy to military age, Isaac was probably an adolescent in this story.

12

"Obey God"—in other translations, "fear God," implying a reverent trust in God that comes out of commitment to God.

Notes

Philippians 4:11-13 (CEV)

(Paul's letter to the church in Philippi was probably written while he was imprisoned in Rome.)

I am not complaining about having too little. I have learned to be satisfied with whatever I have. I know what it is to be poor or to have plenty, and I have lived under all kinds of conditions. I know what it means to be full or to be hungry, to have too much or too little. Christ gives me the strength to face anything.

Pray For

Next Meeting at

_____

Date

_____

"Your only son"–Technically, Abraham had an older son, Ishmael, whose mother had been Sarah's servant. (It was an ancient custom that a wife could allow a servant to bear a child for her husband.) Muslim Arabs trace their ancestry back to Abraham by identifying themselves as descendants of Ishmael. Isaac, however, is called the "only son" in this passage, because it was his birth to Sarah that fulfilled God's promise.

R & R
REFLECT AND RESPOND

Read the Genesis passage. Then reread it, imagining yourself as one of the accompanying servants. Imagine that, instead of staying behind with the other servant, you secretly followed Abraham and Isaac. What did you see and hear? What did you think was going on? How did it make you feel? What questions did you have? What conclusions did you reach? How did you feel about Abraham afterward? about his God?

Read the Genesis passage twice more. Put yourself in the place of Abraham then in the place of Isaac. With each role, note what thoughts and feelings you had. How were you affected? How was your faith affected in the two roles?

Who or what is your "Isaac"? (The person or thing you love more than anything.) Have you offered it or given it to God? Why, or why not? What do you think would happen if you did?

Read Philippians 4:11-13. Verse 13 ("Christ gives me the strength to face anything"). You may want to memorize this verse. Copy it onto a piece of paper and put it where you'll see it frequently. Say it to yourself throughout the day.

Reread Philippians 4:11-13. In what ways have you experienced hardship? contentment? What is one thing you need Christ's strength to face?

What a Hypocrite!

Matthew 7:1-5 (NIV)

(Jesus is teaching his disciples and the crowds.)

"Do not judge, or you too will be judged. For in the same way you judge others, you will be judged, and with the measure you use, it will be measured to you.

"Why do you look at the speck of sawdust in someone else's eye and pay no attention to the plank in your own eye? How can you say to [someone else], 'Let me take the speck out of your eye,' when all the time there is a plank in your own eye? You hypocrite, first take the plank out of your own eye, and then you will see clearly to remove the speck from [the other person's] eye."

Isaiah 58:3-10 (NCV)

(The prophet Isaiah speaks to the nation of Israel, on behalf of God.)

"They say, 'To honor you we had special days when we gave up eating, but you didn't see. We humble ourselves to honor you, but you didn't notice.' " But the LORD says, "You do what pleases yourselves . . . , and you are unfair to your workers. On these special days when you do not eat, you argue and fight and hit each other with your fists. You cannot do these things as you do now and believe your prayers are heard in heaven. This kind of special day is not what I want. This is not the way I want people to be sorry for what they have done. I don't want people just to bow their heads like a plant and wear rough cloth and lie in ashes to show their sadness. This is what you do on your special days when you do not eat, but do you think this is what the LORD wants?

"I will tell you the kind of special day I want: Free the people you have put in prison unfairly and undo their chains. Free those to whom you are unfair and stop their hard labor. Share your food with the hungry and bring poor, homeless people into your own homes. When you see someone who has no clothes, give him yours, and don't refuse to help your own relatives. Then your light will shine like the dawn, and your wounds will quickly heal. Your God will walk before you, and the glory of the LORD will protect you from behind. Then you will call out and the LORD will answer. You will cry out, and he will say, 'Here I am.'

"If you stop making trouble for others, if you stop using cruel words and pointing your finger at others, if you feed those who are hungry and take care of the needs of those who are troubled, then your light will shine in the darkness, and you will be bright like the sunshine at noon."

Wearing sackcloth or covering your body with ashes or dirt were ways of expressing sorrow.

Notes

Pray for

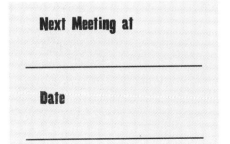

Next Meeting at

_____

Date

_____

R & R
REFLECT AND RESPOND

Read the passage from Matthew. If Jesus were saying these words directly to you, to what specific "plank(s)" would he be referring? Make an honest, prayerful assessment of your own sins. In terms of "planks," would you have a few boards, a pile of them, or a whole lumber yard? Sketch out something you could build with the number of planks you need to remove from your own eye.

Find a piece of wood or a board about a foot long and a few inches wide. (Cardboard works too.) Place one or more candles on it. You may add designs, words, a cross, or anything else to make it an altar and a useful tool for prayer and meditation, as well as a reminder of your own sinfulness and need for forgiveness. Find a permanent spot for it or bring it out as needed.

Write down the name of one or two persons whom you've unfairly judged. Pray for them every day this week, as well as for God to change your judgmental attitude into a loving one.

Light a candle, to symbolize the light and love of God breaking through the darkness of our world. Read Isaiah 58:1-10 several times, slowly, and meditatively. Spend time in prayerful silence. What is God calling you to change in your life? How is God specifically calling you to be a light in the darkness?

PAINTED-ON FAITH

—Britt Cox, 17, Bedford, Texas

I was sitting in church, and a young couple seated behind me was having a discussion during the sermon. I became rather agitated, because they were talking about what they were going to do for lunch. As the sermon went on, I became more angry and more aware of what they were saying than what the minister was saying. I also noticed that when the minister made eye contact with them or the offering plate was passed, the couple would put on their "church faces." I found this so hypocritical and two-faced.

"I would never do such a thing," I thought. But the more I reflected on it, the more guilty I realized I was. I remembered times when I gave advice to friends about getting along with their siblings, then five minutes later, arguing with my own. I remember going to church, not to be with God, but to see that cute boy. I remember praising God's name early Sunday morning and by Monday afternoon, acting like anything but a child of God.

When Jesus called the Pharisees "whitewashed tombs" (Matthew 23:27), he meant they had no spiritual substance—only an exterior appearance. Like the Pharisees, we can be whitewashed and fake. We find the "church face" to wear on Sunday mornings, but on Monday we become our old ugly selves again.

Jesus keeps us real. But if we keep whitewashing or painting over him, it's going to become harder and harder for others to see him in us. With no substance, only a surface, our lives will come crumbling down. But Jesus understands our human hearts. He ate with sinners and hung out with hypocrites. He knows our thoughts, our actions, and motives; but he continues to forgive us. He knows how much we need him. Through his forgiveness, we can become whole again.

Movies that portray high school life often show one of the characters' major temptations being members of the opposite sex. When I was little, I would watch those movies and just laugh, because it was common knowledge that boys had cooties. As I grew up, however, boys became interesting to me. They were intriguing, to say the least. I had always had boundaries as to how far I was willing to go; but the more I went out, the more those boundaries became less firm. I thought that if I gave guys what they wanted, then they would like me more. Needless to say, it didn't work out that way.

To try to understand where to draw the line, I began talking to people about dating and relationships. One of my friends, who is a Christian, told me that it shouldn't be about what I was able to do, but instead, what I wanted to save of myself and keep for that one special person. She also gave me this Bible verse: "Flee from sexual immorality. All other sins a man commits are outside his body, but he who sins sexually sins against his own body. Do you not know that your body is a temple of the Holy Spirit, who is in you, whom you have received from God? You are not your own; you were bought at a price. Therefore honor God with your body" (1 Corinthians 6:18-20, NIV).

Abstaining from sexual immorality is still a struggle for me today, but I have found that surrounding myself with friends who hold me accountable helps me stay on track. We encourage one another to read God's word and to strive to live a Christ-like lifestyle.

HONOR GOD WITH YOUR BODY

—Liz Taber, 16
Ballwin, Missouri

Sleeping With the Enemy

The Book of Judges describes the life and history of the Israelites from the time of Joshua to the time of the monarchy. The stories are about judges, or leaders, chosen by God during this time period, who would save Israel from oppressors. They were not judges such as those in a court of law, but, typically, military leaders.

Judges 16:4-22 (CEV)

Some time later, Samson fell in love with a woman named Delilah. ... The Philistine rulers went to Delilah and said, "Trick Samson into telling you what makes him so strong and what can make him weak. ... If you find out his secret, we will each give you eleven hundred pieces of silver."

The next time Samson was at Delilah's house, she asked, "Samson, what makes you so strong? How can I tie you up so you can't get away? Come on, you can tell me."

Samson answered, "If someone ties me up with seven new bowstrings that have never been dried, it will make me just as weak as anyone else."

The Philistine rulers gave seven new bowstrings to Delilah. They also told some of their soldiers to go to Delilah's house and hide in the room where Samson and Delilah were. ...

Delilah tied up Samson with the bowstrings and shouted, "Samson, the Philistines are attacking!"

Samson snapped the bowstrings, as though they were pieces of scorched string. ...

"You lied and made me look like a fool," Delilah said. "Now tell me. How can I really tie you up?"

Samson answered, "... If I'm tied up with ropes that have never been used, I'll be just as weak as anyone else."

Delilah got new ropes. ... Then she tied up Samson's arms and shouted, "Samson, the Philistines are attacking!"

Samson snapped the ropes as if they were threads.

"You're still lying and making a fool of me," Delilah said. "Tell me how I can tie you up!"

"My hair is in seven braids," Samson replied. "If you weave my braids into the threads on a loom and nail the loom to a wall, then I will be as weak as anyone else."

While Samson was asleep, Delilah wove his braids into the threads on a loom and nailed the loom to a wall. Then she shouted, "Samson, the Philistines are attacking!"

Samson woke up and pulled the loom free. ... Then he pulled his hair free from the woven cloth.

"Samson," Delilah said, "you claim to love me, but you don't mean it! You've made me look like a fool three times now, and you still haven't told me why you are so strong." Delilah started nagging and pestering him day after day, until he couldn't stand it any longer.

Philistines were from Philistia, a confederation of five prosperous cities. They were feared by the Israelites, who considered them tyrants.

Samson was born to a woman who had been unable to have children. He was dedicated to God, as an angel had instructed his parents to do. To stay dedicated to God, Samson had to follow special rules, such as not cutting his hair.

Finally, Samson told her the truth. "I have belonged to God ever since I was born, so my hair has never been cut. If it were ever cut off, my strength would leave me. . . ."

[She lulled him to sleep, cut his hair, accepted the Philistines' money, and then. . .]

Samson woke up and thought, "I'll break loose and escape, just as I always do." He did not realize that the LORD had stopped helping him.

The Philistines grabbed Samson and poked out his eyes. They took him to the prison in Gaza and chained him up. Then they put him to work, turning a millstone to grind grain. But they didn't cut his hair any more, so it started growing back.

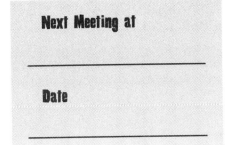

Pray For

Next Meeting at

_____

Date

_____

R & R
REFLECT AND RESPOND

Reread the last three paragraphs of the Judges text (Judges 16:18-22). Samson, although dedicated to God since birth, did most things he did for personal or selfish reasons. Then when he was captured and imprisoned due to his own mistakes, he realized that he could not save himself as he'd been able to in the past. In what ways can you relate, or not relate, to Samson's experience? Have you ever felt that God let you "fall on your face"?

Write down the three most important relationships, dating or friendship, that you're in now. Dedicate them to God. Pray regularly for these relationships. Notice how, over time, giving these relationships to God and praying for them makes a difference.

Galatians 6:7-8 (CEV) says, "You cannot fool God, so don't make a fool of yourself! You will harvest what you plant. If you follow your selfish desires, you will harvest destruction, but if you follow the Spirit, you will harvest eternal life."

Are you currently making a fool of yourself in a relationship? Are you putting yourself at risk emotionally or physically? Are you being deceitful or taking advantage of someone else? What do friends and family members who love you say about the relationships you're in? What might God be saying to you?

Practicing the Presence

Luke 24:13-35 (CEV)

That same day two of Jesus' disciples were going to the village of Emmaus, which was about seven miles from Jerusalem. As they were talking and thinking about what had happened, Jesus came near and started walking along beside them. But they did not know who he was.

Jesus asked them, "What were you talking about as you walked along?"

The two of them stood there looking sad and gloomy. Then the one named Cleopas asked Jesus, "Are you the only person from Jerusalem who didn't know what was happening there these last few days?"

"What do you mean?" Jesus asked.

They answered: "Those things that happened to Jesus of Nazareth. By what he did and said he showed that he was a powerful prophet, who pleased God and all the people. Then the chief priests and our leaders had him arrested and sentenced to die on a cross. We had hoped that he would be the one to set Israel free! But it has already been three days since all this happened.

"Some women in our group surprised us. They had gone to the tomb early in the morning, but did not find the body of Jesus. They came back, saying that they had seen a vision of angels who told them he is alive. Some men from our group went to the tomb and found it just as the women had said. But they didn't see Jesus either."

Then Jesus asked the two disciples, "Why can't you understand? How can you be so slow to believe all that the prophets said? Didn't you know that the Messiah would have to suffer before he was given his glory?" Jesus then explained everything written about himself in the Scriptures, beginning with the Law of Moses and the Books of the Prophets.

When the two of them came near the village where they were going, Jesus seemed to be going farther. They begged him, "Stay with us! It's already late, and the sun is going down." So Jesus went into the house to stay with them.

After Jesus sat down to eat, he took some bread. He blessed and broke it. Then he gave it to them. At once they knew who he was, but he disappeared. They said to each other, "When he talked with us along the road and explained the Scriptures to us, didn't it warm our hearts?" So they got right up and returned to Jerusalem.

The two disciples found the eleven apostles and the others gathered together. And they learned from the group that the Lord was really alive and had appeared to Peter. Then the disciples from Emmaus told what had happened on the road and how they knew he was the Lord when he broke the bread.

20 The two disciples mentioned here were part of the larger following of Jesus and were not part of the twelve, who were closer to Jesus.

"Set Israel free!"—The Jewish nation wanted to be free from bondage to the Roman government and to establish the kingdom of God. They were looking for the Messiah, who would be a political savior.

The town of Emmaus was located on the Jerusalem-to-Joppa road. The ancient road is still used today.

Notes

Pray for

Next Meeting at

_____

Date

_____

R & R
REFLECT AND RESPOND

To create time and space to experience God's presence. Try some of these exercises:

- **journaling**—Write down your thoughts, feelings, questions, and spiritual insights. Note ways God is at work in the lives of others and your own life. Write down prayer requests.
- **being in silence**—Start with a couple of minutes, then try to extend the time. You may want to pick a secluded, quiet place to sit and be silent; or you could be silent on a walk or a bike ride.
- **volunteering**—Do ministry: work in a soup kitchen, tutor a child, visit a nursing home, and so forth.
- **praying the Scriptures**—Read a passage of Scripture several times slowly and prayerfully. What feelings do you have? What words or phrases draw you? What might God be saying to you through the text?
- **being in covenant friendship**—Find a friend (a peer or trusted adult) to pray with or read the Bible with on a regular basis. Share your spiritual insights.

Reread Luke 24:28-35. It seems that Jesus would have kept on walking if the men hadn't invited him to stay. Have you invited Christ to stay with you, or will you let him walk on? Spend a few moments in prayer, inviting him into your life, to stay with you, if you haven't already. Then be ready to encounter his presence in your life.

Ecclesiastes 3:1, 4 (NRSV)

For everything there is a season, and a time for every matter under heaven: . . .
> a time to weep, and a time to laugh.

John 11:17-20, 30-36 (NIV)

On his arrival, Jesus found that Lazarus had already been in the tomb for four days. Bethany was less than two miles from Jerusalem, and many Jews had come to Martha and Mary to comfort them in the loss of their brother. When Martha heard that Jesus was coming, she went out to meet him, but Mary stayed at home.

Now Jesus had not entered the village, but was still at the place where Martha had met him. When the Jews who had been with Mary in the house, comforting her, noticed how quickly she got up and went out, they followed her, supposing she was going to the tomb to mourn there.

When Mary reached the place where Jesus was and saw him, she fell at his feet and said, "Lord, if you had been here, my brother would not have died."

When Jesus saw her weeping, and the Jews who had come along with her also weeping, he was deeply moved in spirit and troubled. "Where have you laid him?" he asked.

"Come and see, Lord," they replied.

Jesus wept.

Then the Jews said, "See how he loved him!"

Romans 12:15 (NIV)

Rejoice with those who rejoice; mourn with those who mourn.

"Jesus wept," John 11:35, is the shortest verse in the Bible.

"Ecclesiastes" is the Greek word for "a teacher who speaks to a large gathering or assembly."

The Book of Ecclesiastes, along with the books of Job and Proverbs, offer reflection and guidance on the human existence; they're known as "Wisdom Books."

If you go to Bethany today, you can visit a 2000-year-old burial site, believed to be Lazarus's tomb.

After four days in the tomb, Lazarus' body would have started to decay; his family and friends would have had no hope of seeing him alive again.

Notes

Pray for

Next Meeting at

_____

Date

_____

R & R
REFLECT AND RESPOND

Read Ecclesiastes 3:1-8. Dig up (from your parents' music collection or on the Internet) the song "Turn, Turn, Turn," music by Pete Seeger, sung by The Byrds. Listen; reflect.

Read the John passage. If you were an actor portraying Jesus or Mary in this scene, what would you think about or do to generate real tears and authentic emotion? (Peeling onions is not allowed!)

What have your parents, or other influential adults, raised you to believe and do, when it comes to showing your emotions, particularly crying? If you had the opportunity to teach a child about showing emotion, would you teach him or her the same thing?

Fill in the blanks:

Crying is _____.
The last time I cried was
_____.
It's not OK to cry when
_____.
It is OK to cry when
_____. When someone I'm around starts crying, I _____.
When I think of Jesus crying, I wonder _____.

I think that if I cried more, I
_____.

When it comes to crying, I wish that I could
_____.

Read Romans 12:15. Write the initials of someone you know who is sad today:
_____. Call or send an encouraging e-mail or card.

Laugh Out Loud

Genesis 17:15-22; 18:1, 10-14; 21:1-6 (NIV)

God also said to Abraham, "As for Sarai your wife, you are no longer to call her Sarai; her name will be Sarah. I will bless her and will surely give you a son by her. I will bless her so that she will be the mother of nations; kings of peoples will come from her."

Abraham fell facedown; he laughed and said to himself, "Will a son be born to a man a hundred years old? Will Sarah bear a child at the age of ninety?" And Abraham said to God, "If only Ishmael might live under your blessing!"

Then God said, "Yes, but your wife Sarah will bear you a son, and you will call him Isaac. I will establish my covenant with him as an everlasting covenant for his descendants after him. And as for Ishmael, I have heard you: I will surely bless him; I will make him fruitful and will greatly increase his numbers. He will be the father of twelve rulers, and I will make him into a great nation. But my covenant I will establish with Isaac, whom Sarah will bear to you by this time next year." When he had finished speaking with Abraham, God went up from him. . . .

The LORD appeared to Abraham near the great trees of Mamre while he was sitting at the entrance to his tent in the heat of the day. . . .

Then the LORD said, "I will surely return to you about this time next year, and Sarah your wife will have a son."

Now Sarah was listening at the entrance to the tent, which was behind him. Abraham and Sarah were already old and well advanced in years, and Sarah was past the age of childbearing. So Sarah laughed to herself as she thought, "After I am worn out and my master is old, will I now have this pleasure?"

Then the LORD said to Abraham, "Why did Sarah laugh and say, 'Will I really have a child, now that I am old?' Is anything too hard for the LORD? I will return to you at the appointed time next year and Sarah will have a son." . . .

Now the LORD was gracious to Sarah as he had said, and the LORD did for Sarah what he had promised. Sarah became pregnant and bore a son to Abraham in his old age, at the very time God had promised him. Abraham gave the name Isaac to the son Sarah bore him. When his son Isaac was eight days old, Abraham circumcised him, as God commanded him. Abraham was a hundred years old when his son Isaac was born to him.

Sarah said, "God has brought me laughter, and everyone who hears about this will laugh with me."

Circumcision is the removal of a male's foreskin, which God commanded that Abraham and his male descendants do as a physical reminder of their commitment to God's covenant.

The Hebrew name "Isaac" means "to laugh."

God changed the name "Abram" ("exalted father") to "Abraham" ("father of a multitude of nations") to confirm Abraham's new role.

Notes

Pray For

Next Meeting at

_____

Date

_____

R & R
REFLECT AND RESPOND

Read the Genesis passage. If you were a reporter, covering this "miraculous" birth story for the local paper, what questions would you ask Abraham, Sarah, and others on the scene? What would the headline be?

How often do you laugh during the average day? Try counting how many times you laugh at something for the next few days, then figure the average: _____.

Whom do you know who needs to lighten up and laugh a little more? Make it a personal goal to get this person to laugh or, at least, to be more positive.

Reread the Genesis passage. What impossibility or obstacle have you experienced in your life that helps you relate to Abraham and Sarah and their astonished disbelief at God's promise to deliver a son? What current impossibility do you need to give over to God?

List three things you laugh at that you shouldn't.

1.

2.

3.

List three things you could laugh about with God.

1.

2.

3.

God's Gift of Laughter

—Cara Martin, 15
Charlotte, North Carolina

My life has always revolved around God. I have grown up as a preacher's daughter and have always been expected to do the right thing. But it's not other people who get me to do right things; it's me. Knowing God has changed me into a person who wants to do right. One thing I have learned over the years is that laughter is a gift from God and is often the right thing to do.

Ecclesiastes 7:13-14 (NIV) says, "Consider what God has done: Who can straighten what he has made crooked? When times are good, be happy; but when times are bad, consider: God has made the one as well as the other." God gave us laughter, because God wants us to be happy and to rejoice about what God does.

Mark Twain once said, "The human race has one really effective weapon, and that is laughter." Laughter can bring your enemies closer to you, and your friends even closer. God has given us a gift—not just Jesus, God's only Son—but God gave us laughter. God wants us to have fun in our lives and wants non-Christians to see how much fun we Christians have.

Just remember to always thank God for giving you this gift, and keep laughing!

y whole life I have been around drinkers, but they are the responsible, occasional drinkers. However, I have also seen many people act violently and irresponsibly because they drank too much alcohol. Alcohol does weird things to the mind and the body. It can scar you internally if you drink too early in life or too much. It can also affect the way others look at you.

God has blessed me with the power to oppose peer pressure. I've been offered alcohol before; but it was easy to reject, with God by my side. It may seem like the world is centered around drugs, crime, and violence; but those are just some things people turn to when they're stressed. God will make you feel stronger, give you hope, and show you that there is somewhere to turn that won't leave you in a hole of neglect.

I was at my friend's house by the lake one night last year. The adults there were all drinking, except one—the designated driver. One of the adults jumped off the dock and onto the boat, causing it to sink. The guy was extremely intoxicated; he was "playing around," as he said. After a while, he chased us through the house. I was scared, because it seemed as if he were trying to harm us. When I tried to escape, he grabbed me and threw me against the wall, then dumped me onto the floor. Luckily, my sister's boyfriend stopped him.

Turning to alcohol to solve problems is a terrible idea. I've seen many things that have made me realize drinking is not for me. God will help you see the light, too!

—Jesse Burgamy, 15
Mooresville, North Carolina

CONTRARY TO THE SPIRIT

Galatians 5:13-26 (NIV)

(This passage is from a letter written by the apostle Paul, reminding Jewish Christians in Galatia that one is made holy, or sanctified, not by legalistic rule-following, but by obedience that comes from faith in God's grace to save and give new life through Jesus Christ.)

You, my brothers [and sisters], were called to be free. But do not use your freedom to indulge the sinful nature; rather, serve one another humbly in love. The entire law is summed up in a single command: "Love your neighbor as yourself." If you keep on biting and devouring each other, watch out or you will be destroyed by each other.

So I say, live by the Spirit, and you will not gratify the desires of the sinful nature. For the sinful nature desires what is contrary to the Spirit, and the Spirit what is contrary to the sinful nature. They are in conflict with each other, so that you do not do what you want. But if you are led by the Spirit, you are not under law.

The acts of the sinful nature are obvious: sexual immorality, impurity and debauchery; idolatry and witchcraft; hatred, discord, jealousy, fits of rage, selfish ambition, dissensions, factions and envy; drunkenness, orgies, and the like. I warn you, as I did before, that those who live like this will not inherit the kingdom of God.

But the fruit of the Spirit is love, joy, peace, patience, kindness, goodness, faithfulness, gentleness and self-control. Against such things there is no law. Those who belong to Christ Jesus have crucified the sinful nature with its passions and desires. Since we live by the Spirit, let us keep in step with the Spirit. Let us not become conceited, provoking and envying each other.

"Led by the Spirit...not under law." Paul's point is that a believer who wants to please God, out of love for God, is empowered by the Spirit to do just that. Otherwise, trying to achieve holiness or earn salvation by just being a rule follower is enslaving and unfulfilling.

Christian virtues, or "fruit," are produced when the Holy Spirit dwells in the life and soul of a believer.

Notes

Pray for

Next Meeting at

_____

Date

_____

R & R
REFLECT AND RESPOND

Think of yourself as a building under construction. The architect and builder is God. Which of the following best describes your project status?

____ Foundation poured;

____ Project on hold, due to resistance by outside parties;

____ Coming along, slowly but surely;

____ Outside looks good, but infrastructure needs major work;

____ Going up nicely, designer/ builder pleased!

Read the passage from Galatians. Jot down what comes to mind as you read through it, especially any questions it raises for you. Pray about them. Talk about your insights and/or questions with a Christian friend, pastor, youth director, or small group leader.

Buy a flowering plant to care for, or start by planting seeds. Give yourself the experience of caring for something that you can watch grow and bloom, like God does with us.

Reread the Galatians passage. As you read it, prayerfully reflect on two or three "fruits" that need to be produced in your life. Highlight or underline them. Ask for God's help daily to grow in those areas. List some specific ways that you can "bear" those "fruits," or virtues in your life this week.

"The Spirit," also known as the Holy Spirit or Holy Ghost, is the Spirit of God, through which humans are empowered to do God's will. The Spirit works with Jesus Christ, bringing us into fellowship with God.

"Entire law" refers to the Hebrew Bible, or Old Testament.

The Party's Over?

In Romans, Paul tells Christians that, even though their choices of what to eat or drink may not affect their faith, they shouldn't do something that would be problematic for another Christian (new convert, someone struggling in his or her faith, one who believes that activity to be sinful, or one who may become addicted).

Proverbs 20:1 (Message)

Wine makes you mean; beer makes you quarrelsome—a staggering drunk is not much fun.

Luke 7:33-34 (NIV)

(Jesus is speaking to the crowd.)

"For John the Baptist came neither eating bread nor drinking wine, and you say, 'He has a demon.' The Son of Man came eating and drinking, and you say, 'Here is a glutton and a drunkard, a friend of tax collectors and "sinners."' But wisdom is proved right by all her children."

1 Peter 4:3-4 (NCV)

In the past you wasted too much time doing what nonbelievers enjoy. You were guilty of sexual sins, evil desires, drunkenness, wild and drunken parties, and hateful idol worship. Nonbelievers think it is strange that you do not do the many wild and wasteful things they do, so they insult you.

Ephesians 5:17—18 (CEV)

Don't be stupid. Instead, find out what the Lord wants you to do. Don't destroy yourself by getting drunk, but let the Spirit fill your life.

1 Timothy 5:23 (CEV)

(Paul is writing to his young friend and colleague, Timothy, who was working at the church in Ephesus.)

Stop drinking only water. Take a little wine to help your stomach trouble and the other illnesses you always have.

Titus 3:1 (Message)

Remind the people to respect the government and be law-abiding, always ready to lend a helping hand.

Romans 14:17, 20-21 (CEV)

God's kingdom isn't about eating and drinking. It is about pleasing God, about living in peace, and about true happiness. . . .

Don't let your appetite destroy what God has done. All foods are fit to eat, but it is wrong to cause problems for others by what you eat. It is best not to eat meat or drink wine or do anything else that causes problems for other followers of the Lord.

1 Corinthians 6:12 (Message)

Just because something is technically legal doesn't mean that it's spiritually appropriate. If I went around doing whatever I thought I could get by with, I'd be a slave to my whims.

Pray for

Next Meeting at

_____

Date

_____

R & R
REFLECT AND RESPOND

On a scale of 1–10 (1 = not a problem; 10 = a huge problem), to what extent is drinking a problem for

___ you
___ your best friends
___ your parents
___ teenagers at your school

If it's a big problem for one or more of those, what can you do about it? Ask God for some direction here.

Read the Bible verses. Search for additional relevant verses if you have a Bible, or do an online search if you can. Spend time in prayer and reflection on this issue. Write a personal statement of belief about drinking. Include what God is calling you, as a teen, to do, as well as what you believe about the use of alcohol, in general.

If you have made a decision not to drink or need to make one, practice how to respond in situations where you will feel pressure to drink.

Reread 1 Corinthians 6:12. Other than drinking, what are some lifestyle choices you make that may be "technically" legal or allowed by parents or friends but not beneficial to you (emotionally, spiritually, and/or physically)? Smoking? drugs? sexual activity? pornography? overeating? pigging out then purging? overspending? over-committing yourself to activities? to others? Have a heart-to-heart talk with God, asking for guidance and strength to make the right choices for you.

Luke 14:25-33 (CEV)

Large crowds were walking along with Jesus, when he turned and said:

"You cannot be my disciple, unless you love me more than you love your father and mother, your wife and children, and your brothers and sisters. You cannot come with me unless you love me more than you love your own life.

"You cannot be my disciple unless you carry your own cross and come with me.

"Suppose one of you wants to build a tower. What is the first thing you will do? Won't you sit down and figure out how much it will cost and if you have enough money to pay for it? Otherwise, you will start building the tower, but not be able to finish. Then everyone who sees what is happening will laugh at you. They will say, 'You started building, but could not finish the job.'

"What will a king do if he has only ten thousand soldiers to defend himself against a king who is about to attack him with twenty thousand soldiers? Before he goes out to battle, won't he first sit down and decide if he can win? If he thinks he won't be able to defend himself, he will send messengers and ask for peace while the other king is still a long way off. So then, you cannot be my disciple unless you give away everything you own."

"Carry your own cross"—In Jesus' time, people condemned to be crucified were forced to carry their cross to the place of crucifixion; symbolically, Jesus is asking his followers for their total commitment to serve God, whatever the cost, for the rest of their lives.

Some translations say "hate his father and mother." This is a form of speech known as hyperbole and is used by Jesus for emphasis, to stress that a follower must love him even more than his or her immediate family.

A "disciple" is a follower.

Notes

Pray for

Next Meeting at

_____

Date

_____

R & R
REFLECT AND RESPOND

What do you believe about Jesus? Jot down statements or words that express what you believe about him. Where do these beliefs come from?

Read the passage from Luke. Imagine that you are in the crowd, listening to Jesus. Later, you run into friends. What do you tell them about what you saw and heard?

You can't love someone you don't know. How well do you know Jesus? If you haven't already, challenge yourself to read one of the Gospels—Matthew, Mark, Luke, or John—over the next few days. If you don't have a Bible translation that's easy to read and understand, borrow one from a friend, the church, or library. Try *The Message,* Contemporary English Version (CEV), or New International Version (NIV).

Find a quiet place where you can spend undisturbed time talking or writing to Jesus. Create some "holy space": light a candle, play music that's spiritually meaningful to you. Invite Christ to make himself known to you. Tell him about your life—the good and the bad. Ask questions. Be still. Let this be the beginning of a personal ritual of spending time with him.

Do you want to move beyond belief? What obstacles are keeping you from following Christ? What do you love more than him? What sacrifices may you need to make?

Give Thanks

Luke 17:11-19 (Message)

It happened that as he made his way toward Jerusalem, he crossed over the border between Samaria and Galilee. As he entered a village, ten men, all lepers, met him. They kept their distance but raised their voices, calling out, "Jesus, Master, have mercy on us!"

Taking a good look at them, he said, "Go, show yourselves to the priests."

They went, and while still on their way, became clean. One of them, when he realized that he was healed, turned around and came back, shouting his gratitude, glorifying God. He kneeled at Jesus' feet, so grateful. He couldn't thank him enough—and he was a Samaritan.

Jesus said, "Were not ten healed? Where are the nine? Can none be found to come back and give glory to God except this outsider?" Then he said to him, "Get up. On your way. Your faith has healed and saved you."

Philippians 1:3-11 (CEV)

(Paul is writing from prison to the church in Philippi, a Roman colony and important city in Macedonia.)

Every time I think of you, I thank my God. And whenever I mention you in my prayers, it makes me happy. This is because you have taken part with me in spreading the good news from the first day you heard about it. God is the one who began this good work in you, and I am certain that [God] won't stop before it is complete on the day that Christ Jesus returns.

You have a special place in my heart. So it is only natural for me to feel the way I do. All of you have helped in the work that God has given me, as I defend the good news and tell about it here in jail. God...knows how much I want to see you. [God] knows that I care for you in the same way that Christ Jesus does.

I pray that your love will keep on growing and that you will fully know and understand how to make the right choices. Then you will still be pure and innocent when Christ returns. And until that day, Jesus Christ will keep you busy doing good deeds that bring glory and praise to God.

Lepers were people who suffered from skin diseases, of which there were a variety. They were considered "unclean," or unacceptable to worship God, and were restricted to isolated places to prohibit contact with other Jews (which would make them unclean).

34 Showing yourself to a Jewish priest was normal procedure after being cured of a skin disease so that he could pronounce you "clean" and reinstate you into the religious and social life of the Jewish community

Notes

Pray for

Next Meeting at

_____

Date

_____

R & R
REFLECT AND RESPOND

Read the Luke passage. Then read it again, trying to recreate in your mind what might have happened. Put yourself in the story, as one of the lepers, as Jesus, or as an onlooker. Where were you; what was the setting? What was the climate? What did the lepers look like? What words were exchanged? What thoughts and feelings might each person have experienced?

Has anything happened to you that caused you to feel the type of gratitude that the leper felt? What has been one thing that you're most grateful for in your life? _____ Have you thanked anyone? God?

Take the "Attitude of Gratitude" Challenge 1: Over the next three days, for everything that goes wrong or disappoints you, find something in the situation for which to be thankful. (Can you keep it up?)

Take the "Attitude of Gratitude" Challenge 2: For the next week, every time you pray for help for yourself or someone else, offer a prayer of thanks for something too.

Read the Philippians passage. Using some of the words and thoughts from this passage, personalize a letter or e-mail to someone who has been helpful and encouraging to you. (If you quote it word for word, be sure to include the Bible reference.)

EXPERIENCING GOD

No two people experience God in exactly the same way. People who attend the same church may worship in the same manner, but their relationship with God may be completely different. Part of this relationship is the way in which God tells us things. I grew up not attending church most Sundays, so I never had a firm sense of what it should be like to experience God.

I sometimes wish that I had the religious background that some of my friends have had. The sense of community that comes from being in a church family is so valuable. However, I am thankful that I have been given the opportunity to create my own relationship with God. Contrary to the thunder-and-lightening effects of the movies, I have always talked with God through the smallest of details. I don't think anyone needs something grandiose to have a spiritual experience. Walking outside, observing the intricacies of nature, listening to a moving piece of music, capturing a moment in time with a photograph—these are the small ways in which I feel I communicate directly with God. Noticing these things, for me, is God's way of telling me, "Slow down, enjoy life!"

I believe that to be truly connected with God, we need to see God's work in everything around us—not just in church on Sundays. In the words of J. Krishnamurti, "You must understand the whole of life, not just one little part of it. That is why you must read; that is why you must look at the skies; that is why you must sing, and dance, and suffer and write poems and understand—for all that is life."

—Sarah Lee, 18
Charlotte, North Carolina

American society does have an official religion, but it is not Christianity, Judaism, Islam, or Buddhism. Our country's religion is consumerism. The desire to have and buy everything we see is the foundation, we believe, of our prosperity. Advertising is one of America's largest industries. Even Christians celebrate the birth of Christ by spending millions of dollars for gifts. The "American Dream" is about becoming wealthy—about having the best car, house, or clothes. We foolishly believe that we are validated if we achieve this dream, that having more will make others and ourselves think that we are "better" people.

This culture of materialism influences everyone and permeates every part of our lives, even our relationship with God. We are so overcome with this desire to have more, be more, and own more, that we often have the audacity to turn to God and expect God to just give it to us. Christians ask God to give us things because we've "been good" or we "promise to be good from now on if. ..." It's as if God is nothing more than a Santa Claus.

Our prayers ought to be of praise and thanks to God. Look around at the world that God has created and given to us. God has given us the freedom to choose our actions yet still promises to always love and forgive us, no matter how immoral or misguided our choices may be. God has given us the gift of eternal life through Christ and promises us an eternity of sublime ecstasy. These gifts are priceless. We ought to spend all our lifetime thanking God for all God has given us. Having an attitude of gratitude to God means never forgetting that God has given us more than we ever deserved and more than we can ever repay. It means saying thanks in all our prayers and in all our thoughts.

—Nathan Hopkins, 17
Ballwin, Missouri

AN ATTITUDE OF GRATITUDE

Lethal Weapon

It's believed that the Book of James was written by James, the brother of Jesus. James was a major leader in the early Christian church. At first, James didn't believe in Jesus' mission or that he was God's son.

James 3:2-10 (Message)

If you could find someone whose speech was perfectly true, you'd have a perfect person, in perfect control of life.

A bit in the mouth of a horse controls the whole horse. A small rudder on a huge ship in the hands of a skilled captain sets a course in the face of the strongest winds. A word out of your mouth may seem of no account, but it can accomplish nearly anything—or destroy it!

It only takes a spark, remember, to set off a forest fire. A careless or wrongly placed word out of our mouth can do that. By our speech we can ruin the world, turn harmony to chaos, throw mud on a reputation, send the whole world up in smoke and go up in smoke with it, smoke right from the pit of hell.

This is scary: You can tame a tiger, but you can't tame a tongue—it's never been done. The tongue runs wild, a wanton killer. With our tongues we bless God our Father; with the same tongues we curse the very men and women [God] made in his image. Curses and blessings out of the same mouth!

My friends, this can't go on.

Ephesians 4:29, 31-32 (NIV)

Do not let any unwholesome talk come out of your mouths, but only what is helpful for building others up according to their needs, that it may benefit those who listen. . . . Get rid of all bitterness, rage and anger, brawling and slander, along with every form of malice. Be kind and compassionate to one another, forgiving each other, just as in Christ God forgave you.

Matthew 8:5-8, 13, 16 (NIV)

When Jesus had entered Capernaum, a centurion came to him asking for help. "Lord," he said, "my servant lies at home paralyzed, suffering terribly."

Jesus said to him, "I will go and heal him."

The centurion replied, "Lord, I do not deserve to have you come under my roof. But just say the word, and my servant will be healed. . . .

Then Jesus said to the centurion, "Go! Let it be done just as you believed it would." And his servant was healed at that very hour. . . .

When evening came, many who were demon-possessed were brought to [Jesus], and he drove out the spirits with a word and healed all the sick.

A "centurion" was a Roman military officer.

Capernaum was a large, busy town that was home base for Jesus during his ministry in Galilee, one of the three provinces of Palestine. It was the center of the fishing industry and the home of Jesus' disciples who were fishermen, like Peter.

Notes

Pray for

Next Meeting at

_____

Date

_____

R & R
REFLECT AND RESPOND

Read the Bible passages from James, Ephesians, and Matthew. Pick one of the passages to reread. Before reading it, ask God to speak to you through the text. Read the passage slowly two or three times. Make notes on what you think God is saying to you in these verses.

Which of the following best describes your tongue (use of words)? If you'd like, draw a picture to illustrate your choice.

a. a wild animal, totally untamed and uncontrollable
b. a spark that burns others
c. a mudslinger
d. an encourager
e. a healer

What is one thing you promise to work on this coming week, with regard to your mouth and the words you use? Be specific. (And ask your other small group members how they're doing with what they promised to do.)

"Cold words freeze people, and hot words scorch them, and bitter words make them bitter, and wrathful words make them wrathful. Kind words also produce their image on men's souls; and a beautiful image it is. They smooth, and quiet, and comfort the hearer."

—Blaise Paschal

A Strange Thing Happened

Numbers 22:22-35 (CEV)

Balaam was riding his donkey to Moab, and two of his servants were with him. But God was angry that Balaam had gone, so one of the LORD's angels stood in the road to stop him. When Balaam's donkey saw the angel standing there with a sword, it walked off the road and into an open field. Balaam had to beat the donkey to get it back on the road.

Then the angel stood between two vineyards, in a narrow path with a stone wall on each side. When the donkey saw the angel, it walked so close to one of the walls that Balaam's foot scraped against the wall. Balaam beat the donkey again.

The angel moved once more and stood in a spot so narrow that there was no room for the donkey to go around. So it just lay down. Balaam lost his temper, then picked up a stick and smacked the donkey.

When that happened, the LORD told the donkey to speak, and it asked Balaam, "What have I done to you that made you beat me three times?"

"You made me look stupid!" Balaam answered. "If I had a sword, I'd kill you here and now!"

"But you're my owner," replied the donkey, "and you've ridden me many times. Have I ever done anything like this before?"

"No," Balaam admitted.

Just then, the LORD let Balaam see the angel standing in the road, holding a sword, and Balaam bowed down.

The angel said, "You had no right to treat your donkey like that! I was the one who blocked your way, because I don't think you should go to Moab. If your donkey had not seen me and stopped those three times, I would have killed you and let the donkey live."

Balaam replied, "I was wrong. I didn't know you were trying to stop me. If you don't think I should go, I'll return home right now."

"It's all right for you to go," the LORD's angel answered. "But you must say only what I tell you." So Balaam went on with Balak's officials.

Balaam was a non-Israelite prophet who worshiped God but dabbled in the occult (forbidden by Hebrew law). Balaam was hired by King Balak to curse Israel. God became angry when Balaam chose money over serving God.

40 Moab was a nation east of the Dead Sea, whose people were descended from Lot, Abraham's nephew.

R & R
REFLECT AND RESPOND

Crunch some Numbers. If you have access to a Bible (preferably a youth-friendly version, such as *The Message,* NIV, CEV, or *The Living Bible*) or a Bible website (such as www.gateway.com), read a fuller account of the story of Balaam and the donkey, Numbers 22— 24. Find out how the story ends.

Read Numbers 22:22-35 again. Balaam's ability to deliver blessings and curses was a gift from God, whom he worshiped. While Balaam is on his way to deliver a curse in exchange for money, God intervenes in a dramatic way so that Balaam would use his gift for God's purposes instead. What gift or ability do you have that God wants you to use for God's purposes, rather than your own?

Find a small, hard object, such as a stone, golf ball, or bead. Hold it in your hand and let it symbolize something in your life that you're stubborn about or unwilling to change although you feel God's urging to do so. This could be a bad habit, a grudge, an attitude, a relationship, or so forth. After praying about it with God, leave the object in a visible place as a reminder and an encouragement.

Who do you know who's headed for trouble and needs "a donkey," or obstacle, stuck in the way? How may God want to use you to get his or her attention?

Holy Ghost, Batman!

John 14:23-26 (NIV)

(Jesus is speaking to his disciples before his arrest and crucifixion.)

Jesus replied, "If anyone loves me, he will obey my teaching. My Father will love him, and we will come to him and make our home with him. He who does not love me will not obey my teaching. These words you hear are not my own; they belong to the Father who sent me. All this I have spoken while still with you. But the Counselor, the Holy Spirit, whom the Father will send in my name, will teach you all things and will remind you of everything I have said to you."

Acts 2:1-6, 14-17, 36-38 (NIV)

When the day of Pentecost came, they were all together in one place. Suddenly a sound like the blowing of a violent wind came from heaven and filled the whole house where they were sitting. They saw what seemed to be tongues of fire that separated and came to rest on each of them. All of them were filled with the Holy Spirit and began to speak in other tongues as the Spirit enabled them.

Now there were staying in Jerusalem God-fearing Jews from every nation under heaven. When they heard this sound, a crowd came together in bewilderment, because each one heard them speaking in his own language. . . .

Then Peter stood up with the Eleven, raised his voice and addressed the crowd: "Fellow Jews and all of you who live in Jerusalem, let me explain this to you; listen carefully to what I say. These men are not drunk, as you suppose. It's only nine in the morning! No, this is what was spoken by the prophet Joel:

" 'In the last days, God says, "I will pour out my Spirit on all people. Your sons and daughters will prophesy, your young men will see visions, your old men will dream dreams." ' " . . .

"Therefore let all Israel be assured of this: God has made this Jesus, whom you crucified, both Lord and Christ."

When the people heard this, they were cut to the heart and said to Peter and the other apostles, "Brothers, what shall we do?"

Peter replied, "Repent and be baptized, every one of you, in the name of Jesus Christ for the forgiveness of your sins. And you will receive the gift of the Holy Spirit."

Pentecost was originally a Jewish festival held 50 days after Passover to celebrate the wheat harvest. For Christians, Pentecost is observed as the day the Holy Spirit was given to the followers of Christ.

1 John 4:12-16 (Message)

(First John was a letter to some of the early Christians, written by John, Jesus' disciple and writer of the Gospel of John.)

No one has seen God, ever. But if we love one another, God dwells deeply within us, and [God's] love becomes complete in us—perfect love!

This is how we know we're living steadily and deeply in [God], and he in us: He's given us life from his life, from his very own Spirit. Also, we've seen for ourselves and continue to state openly that the Father sent his son as Savior of the world. Everyone who confesses that Jesus is God's Son participates continuously in an intimate relationship with God. We know it so well, we've embraced it heart and soul, this love that comes from God.

Pray for

R & R
REFLECT AND RESPOND

When you hear the words "Holy Spirit" or "Holy Ghost," what visual image do you get? a flame of fire? smoke? a dove? a super hero? Casper the Friendly Ghost? leaves rustled by the wind? other? (Feel free to sketch it.)

Read the verses from Acts. Write one or two newspaper headlines that would best capture what happened that wild and crazy day.

Read 1 John 4:12-16. Then, talk to a Christian friend, relative, or pastor about the Holy Spirit. Share your questions. How does that person explain it? How has that person experienced it?

Read John 14:23-26. Has Jesus Christ made his home in you? Which areas of your life does he still need to enter? List one or two of his teachings that you need the Spirit's help to follow.

KUDZU

Psalm 119:9-15, 29-32, 105, 110-112 (Message)

How can a young person live a clean life?
    By carefully reading the map of your Word.
I'm single-minded in pursuit of you;
    don't let me miss the road signs you've posted.
I've banked your promises in the vault of my heart
    so I won't sin myself bankrupt.
Be blessed, God;
    train me in your ways of wise living.
I'll transfer to my lips
    all the counsel that comes from your mouth;
I delight far more in what you tell me about living
    than in gathering a pile of riches.
I ponder every morsel of wisdom from you,
    I attentively watch how you've done it. . . .
Barricade the road that goes Nowhere;
    grace me with your clear revelation.
I choose the true road to Somewhere,
    I post your road signs at every curve and corner.
I grasp and cling to whatever you tell me;
    GOD, don't let me down!
I'll run the course you lay out for me
    if you'll just show me how. . . .
By your words I can see where I'm going;
    they throw a beam of light on my dark path. . . .
The wicked do their best to throw me off track,
    but I don't swerve an inch from your course.
I inherited your book on living; it's mine forever—
    what a gift! And how happy it makes me!
I concentrate on doing exactly what you say—
    I always have and always will.

John 8:31-32 (CEV)

Jesus told the people who had faith in him, "If you keep on obeying what I have said, you truly are my disciples. You will know the truth, and the truth will set you free."

A "disciple" is someone who learns from or follows the teachings of another, often referring to one who follows Jesus Christ.

"Truth," here, means the truth that leads to salvation, rather than philosophical truth. "Free" refers to freedom from sin, not ignorance.

A "psalm" is a song of praise, particularly that found in the Hebrew scriptures, or Old Testament.

Notes

Pray for

Next Meeting at

_____

Date

_____

R & R
REFLECT AND RESPOND

Read the verses from Psalm 119. Highlight or underline words or phrases that you find most meaningful or challenging.

Reread the verses from Psalm 119. Draw a road map of your life, indicating times or places where there were road signs (what were they?); draw and label the roads to "Nowhere" and "Somewhere" (what were they for you?); where did "the wicked" try to throw you off course (and how?); identify some of the curves and the places where it was dark (why?).

Lectio divina is a spiritual practice of reading (*lectio*) and praying the Scripture—another helpful piece of gear for the road! Try it out with John 8:31-32.

• First, find a quiet, undisturbed place. Relax and slow your breathing.

• Read the verses slowly and reverently, listening intently for what God may be saying to you. Do this more than once.

• Then meditate on what you have read; ponder it, think about it with your heart.

• Then pray it; talk to God about what you've been thinking or feeling; repeat a verse or phrase several times as a prayer.

• Finally, be still in God's presence. Let God embrace you and fill you.

Group Members

Leader:_____ Phone: _____
E-mail: _____

Leader:_____ Phone: _____
E-mail: _____

Counselor: _____ Phone: _____
E-mail: _____

Counselor: _____ Phone: _____
E-mail: _____

_____ Phone: _____
Address:_____
_____
E-mail: _____

_____ Phone: _____
Address:_____
_____
E-mail: _____

_____ Phone: _____
Address:_____
_____
E-mail: _____

_____ Phone: _____
Address:_____
_____
E-mail: _____

_____ Phone: _____

Address:_____

_____

E-mail: _____

_____ Phone: _____

Address:_____

_____

E-mail: _____

_____ Phone: _____

Address:_____

_____

E-mail: _____

_____ Phone: _____

Address:_____

_____

E-mail: _____

_____ Phone: _____

Address:_____

_____

E-mail: _____

_____ Phone: _____

Address:_____

_____

E-mail: _____

_____ Phone: _____

Address:_____

_____

E-mail: _____

SYNAGO

Synago (syn-AH-go) is the Greek word for "come together." It is the root word of "synagogue" a place were people come together to worship and to learn the life-giving faith. In Synago, you too will find a place among friends who come together to worship and to learn.

"Synago" also means "to take in." You know who's seeking, who's struggling, who's in need of God's love. Invite them, and let the Synago group take them in with love.

"Synago" is also the root word of "synergy," where the coming together of individual parts makes something even greater. And so it is in Synago. In coming together to talk about your lives in light of God's good news, you will find that something great happens.

Welcome to Synago.